LIFE ON THE TRAIL

Bobbie Kalman

Crabtree Publishing Company

LIFE IN THE OLD WEST

Created by Bobbie Kalman

To Grant Calder
A true trail blazer

Author and Editor-in-Chief
Bobbie Kalman

Managing editor
Lynda Hale

Senior editor
April Fast

Research and editing team
Kate Calder
John Crossingham
Heather Levigne
Hannelore Sotzek
Marsha Baddeley

Computer design
Lynda Hale
Robert MacGregor (cover concept)
Campbell Creative Services

Photo research
Kate Calder
Heather Levigne

Production coordinator
Hannelore Sotzek

Special thanks to
Jerri Stone, National Cowboy Hall of Fame; Hugh A. Dempsey

Photographs and reproductions
Montana Historical Society, Helena: pages 28 (bottom),
    29 (top right); L.A. Huffman: pages 19, 28 (top), 29 (top left)
National Cowboy Hall of Fame, Oklahoma City: pages 26, 27,
    28 (middle), 29 (bottom); William Robinson Leigh,
    Branding JJ (detail): pages 8-9
Inga Spence/The Picture Cube: page 10 (bottom)
The Stock Solution: David Stoecklein: title page, pages 10 (top),
    12, 21, 24, 30; Doug Wilson: page 31
Other images by Digital Vision and Image Club Graphics

Illustrations
Barbara Bedell: pages 9, 11 (horse head), 12, 14-15, 18-19, 20-21
Bonna Rouse: back cover, pages 7, 17, 22-23, 25, 30, lasso border
    throughout book

Separations and film
Dot 'n Line Image Inc.; CCS Princeton (cover)

Printer
Worzalla Publishing Company

Crabtree Publishing Company

350 Fifth Avenue	360 York Road, RR 4	73 Lime Walk
Suite 3308	Niagara-on-the-Lake	Headington
New York	Ontario, Canada	Oxford OX3 7AD
N.Y. 10118	L0S 1J0	United Kingdom

Cataloging in Publication Data
Kalman, Bobbie
    Life on the trail

(Life in the Old West)
Includes index.

ISBN 0-7787-0072-0 (library bound) ISBN 0-7787-0104-2 (pbk.)
This book describes the life and work of cowboys, including the
roundup, branding, bronco busting, and driving cattle hundreds of
miles along cattle trails.

1. Ranch life—West (North America)—History—19th century—
Juvenile literature. 2. Cattle trails—West (North America)—
History—19th century—Juvenile literature. 3. West (North
America)—Social life and customs—Juvenile literature. I. Title.
II. Series: Kalman, Bobbie. Life in the Old West.

F596.K355 1999   j978'.02   LC 98-40378
                                                              CIP

TABLE OF CONTENTS

THE TRAIL DRIVE

In the 1500s, Spanish settlers came to North America. Some of them settled in the southwestern regions that are now Texas and California. They brought horses and longhorn cattle with them. They raised the cattle for their hides and **tallow**, or fat. The cattle and horses roamed free, grazing on the land. These hardy animals quickly grew in number. Soon millions of cattle roamed the **open range**.

Ranching for beef

By the 1820s, many American settlers moved west to become ranchers. The newcomers saw a great business opportunity in gathering the longhorn cattle and selling it to markets in the east. Getting the beef from the west to the east, however, presented a challenge!

Taking the cattle to market

Since there was no refrigeration in the 1800s, the cattle had to be taken live to the cities. If the cattle were slaughtered in Texas, the meat would spoil by the time it reached New York. The cattle could be transported by train part of the way, but first they had to be walked to the nearest railway station. The towns with railway stations became known as **cattle towns**.

Driving the cattle

Ranchers hired cowboys to guide the cattle on the long walk to the cattle towns. The walk was known as a **cattle drive**, or **trail drive**. Most trail drives headed east to cattle towns in Missouri and Kansas. Some drives, however, went north to stock Canadian ranches with cattle.

The trail drive was hundreds of miles long and lasted from three weeks to three months. From sunrise to sunset, cowboys on horseback drove the cattle along the trail. Many of the cattle trails crossed Native territories.

Different cultures

The cowboys who drove the cattle came from many cultures. Some of the cowboys were Americans from the east, and others were immigrants from European countries. More than one-quarter of the cowboys were African Americans. Many had been slaves working on **plantations**, or large farms, in the south and knew how to handle animals.

Native American cowboys

Native Americans also became cowboys. The Spanish and Mexican ranchers had taught them riding and roping skills. Native cowboys were helpful on trail drives because they were able to talk with other Native Americans, who charged a fee to cross over their land.

The *vaqueros*

Many Mexican cowboys worked on the trail drives. Mexican cowboys were called *vaqueros*. *Vaquero* means cowboy. In Spanish, the letter *v* is pronounced as *b*. Early American cowboys called themselves "buckaroos" because that is how they pronounced *vaqueros*.

The *vaqueros* were descendants of the Spanish and Native Americans. They taught the early American ranchers how to ride horses and herd and rope cattle. *Vaqueros* wore wide-brimmed hats called *sombreros*. Cowboys started wearing similar hats to protect their head from the hot sun. The *vaqueros* also introduced cowboys to a different type of saddle that was better for roping cattle.

The Chisholm Trail and the Texas Fever

Many trails led to the cattle towns, but the most famous was the Chisholm Trail. It was named after an early settler, Jesse Chisholm, who created a wagon trail in the mid-1800s. At first, this trail was used for trading, but the cattle drivers extended it in later years to reach **railhead** towns in Kansas. Abilene, Ellsworth, and Dodge City were railhead towns.

Safe driving

The Chisholm Trail was popular—in five years cowboys used the trail to drive over a million cattle to railheads. Cowboys liked this trail because it was straight and flat. There were fewer hills and forests where coyotes or rustlers could hide to attack or steal the cattle. Rivers along the Chisholm Trail were also easier to **ford**, or cross, than rivers on other trails.

Paying for passage

The Chisholm Trail went directly through Oklahoma and across land occupied by Native American Nations such as the Cherokee and Comanche. The trail boss paid Native Americans a fee for the right to cross their land and to allow the cattle to **graze**, or feed.

The Texas fever

The Chisholm Trail became more popular because of a disease called the **Texas fever**. The Texas fever was caused by small insects called ticks. Although longhorn cattle from Texas carried these pests, the ticks did not make them sick. The cattle in the northern states, however, were a different type of cattle. They were not as hardy as the longhorns. Many northern cattle died because they caught the Texas fever from ticks carried by the longhorns.

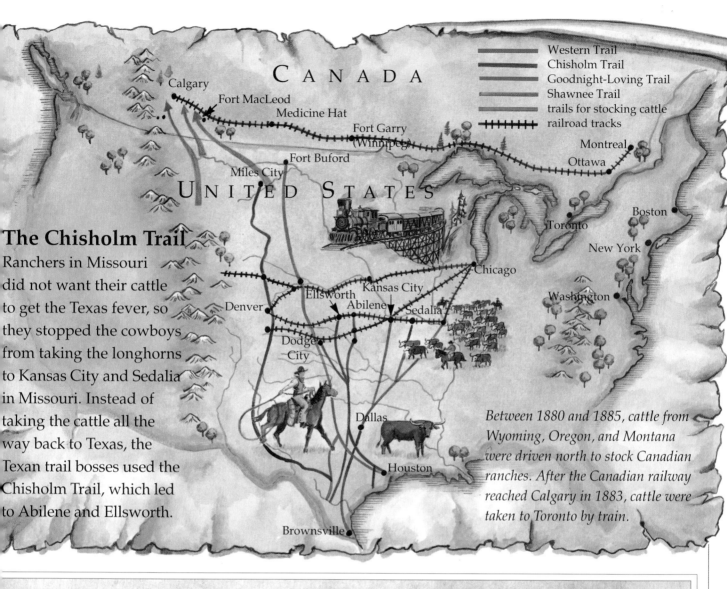

CANADA

Calgary
Fort MacLeod
Medicine Hat
Fort Garry
(Winnipeg)
Montreal
Ottawa
Fort Buford
Miles City

UNITED STATES

Boston

Toronto

New York

The Chisholm Trail

Ranchers in Missouri did not want their cattle to get the Texas fever, so they stopped the cowboys from taking the longhorns to Kansas City and Sedalia in Missouri. Instead of taking the cattle all the way back to Texas, the Texan trail bosses used the Chisholm Trail, which led to Abilene and Ellsworth.

Chicago

Ellsworth
Kansas City
Abilene
Denver
Sedalia
Washington

Dodge
City

Dallas

Houston

Between 1880 and 1885, cattle from Wyoming, Oregon, and Montana were driven north to stock Canadian ranches. After the Canadian railway reached Calgary in 1883, cattle were taken to Toronto by train.

Brownsville

Western Trail
Chisholm Trail
Goodnight-Loving Trail
Shawnee Trail
trails for stocking cattle
railroad tracks

ROUNDUP AND BRANDING

Cattle ranches were built on the unsettled grassland of the western plains called the open range. Ranches were many miles apart with huge areas between them. Cattle grazed freely over this open range all winter and often roamed great distances. Cattle from different ranches grazed together.

Before a herd could be driven on the trail to a cattle town, the cattle had to be **rounded up**, or gathered. Roundup time was twice a year, in the spring and fall. Cattle were often so far from the ranch that cowboys had to camp out on the range while they rounded up the herd.

Separating the herds

During roundup, cowboys checked the brands on the cattle. Cattle from other ranches were returned to their owners. Once herds from different ranches were separated, cattle that were big enough to be sold for meat were sorted and counted. Calves born during the winter were branded, too.

Cowboys roped and dragged new calves away from the rest of the herd. Two cowboys held a calf down while another quickly branded its hide. After it was branded, the calf was released to scurry back to its mother.

Branding

Ranchers **branded**, or marked, their cattle with a symbol of their ranch. The brand helped identify their animals. Each ranch had its own symbol. Branding was done by heating a **branding iron** over a fire pit. A branding iron is a long metal bar with a symbol at one end. Cowboys held the animal down and burned the symbol into its hide. Branding helped ranchers identify their animals. It also discouraged thieves from stealing the cattle.

Can you identify these brands?
- *the triple K*
- *the double diamond*
- *the turkey track*
- *the bow and arrow*

Bronco Busting

Horses were very important to cowboys on the trail. Strong horses helped them drive cattle hundreds of miles. The cowboys rode on horseback all day. Horses also pulled the chuck wagon, which carried food and supplies.

Wild horses

Wild horses were called **broncos**. Ranchers hired cowboys called **bronco busters** to capture and tame wild horses. Catching broncos was a difficult and dangerous task because these horses were not used to being around people. They had never been ridden before.

*Cowboys caught a bronco by throwing a **lariat**, or lasso, around the horse's neck. A lariat is a long rope with a loop at one end. Once the bronco was lassoed, the other end of the rope was tied to a post to keep the horse from running away.*

The first lassos were made by the *vaqueros*, who braided strips of cow rawhide to form a long rope. Years later, cowboys made lassos from tough hemp fibers. Rope made from hemp was strong, stiff, and easy to throw at a target.

Busting a bronco

Broncos that had just been caught were too wild to be useful. They had to be **busted** or **broken**. To break a horse means to tame it. When the bronco was caught and ready to be broken, the bronco buster put a **bridle**, or harness, on its head. He also put a blanket and saddle on the horse's back. The wool blanket prevented the saddle from rubbing against the horse's hide and causing sores.

Bucking bronco!

A bronco did not like a bridle on its head, a saddle on its back, or a rope around its neck. It certainly did not want a cowboy on its back! The wild horse kicked, snorted, bucked, and jumped. The more the horse bucked, the rougher the cowboy treated it. Cowboys used a lariat, spurs, and a **quirt**, or whip, to control a bronco. These tools helped bronco busters break horses quickly. The more horses cowboys broke, the more money ranchers paid them. Broncos that were busted were called **cow ponies**.

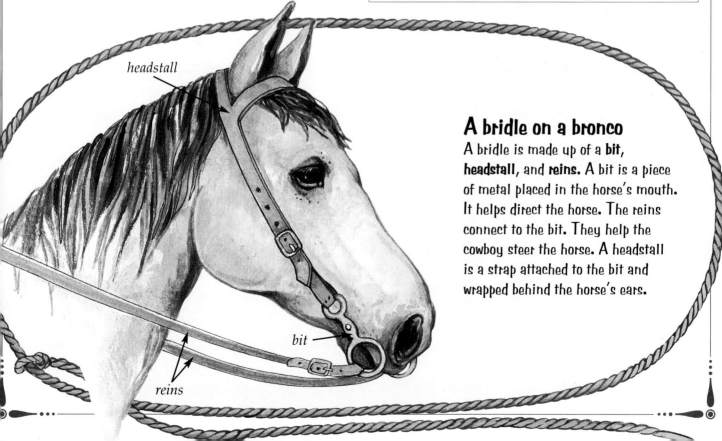

headstall

bit

reins

A bridle on a bronco
A bridle is made up of a **bit**, **headstall**, and **reins**. A bit is a piece of metal placed in the horse's mouth. It helps direct the horse. The reins connect to the bit. They help the cowboy steer the horse. A headstall is a strap attached to the bit and wrapped behind the horse's ears.

When the cattle and horses were ready to be taken on the trail drive, cowboys packed their equipment. The rancher owned the cattle and horses that went on the trail drive. The cowboy owned only a few items.

Packing their tools

A cowboy had to carry most of his belongings on a single horse. To avoid tiring the horse, the cowboy carried only what was necessary. **Saddlebags** tied beneath the **cantle** held small items. The cowboy's bedroll was fastened with twine above the saddlebags or carried on the chuck wagon. Ropes were tied to the saddle with leather straps.

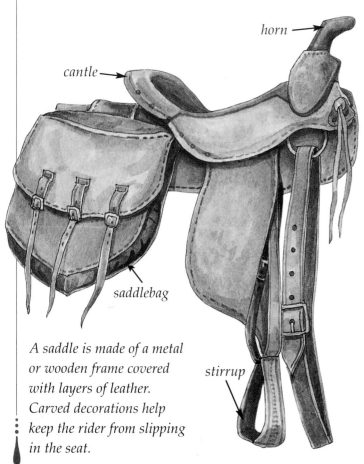

horn

cantle

saddlebag

stirrup

A saddle is made of a metal or wooden frame covered with layers of leather. Carved decorations help keep the rider from slipping in the seat.

A good saddle

A cowboy had to buy his own saddle. It was the most important piece of equipment he owned. He sat in the saddle at least fifteen hours a day, so he had to be sure it was strong and comfortable. A good saddle cost a month's wages, but it lasted thirty years or more.

Self defense

Cowboys carried guns on the trail, but they did not use them often. Bullets were expensive, so cowboys did not shoot unless it was necessary. A gun was often a cowboy's only defense against dangers on the trail, such as rattlesnakes and coyotes.

Everything was useful

Since cowboys brought very little with them on the trail drive, every piece of clothing they wore had to be useful.

A cowboy's hat protected him from rain, sun, and snow. He used his hat to carry water and food to his horse or to fan campfires.

Shirts were made of long-lasting material such as wool or heavy cotton. They were often worn with a vest that had many pockets.

Cowboys used bandannas to wipe sweat away and keep dust out of their mouth and nose.

*Leather **chaps** protected trousers from being torn by scrub brush, cacti, or cattle horns.*

*Cowboys wore one-piece wool underwear called **long johns** beneath their clothes to help them stay warm at night.*

Trousers made of wool were hot and wore out quickly. In the 1870s, cowboys began wearing pants made of denim. Cowboys did not wear belts, so their pants had to fit snugly.

Leather boots protected a cowboy's feet. The narrow-toed boots slid in and out of stirrups easily. High heels kept the boot from slipping out of the stirrup.

Spurs were small, spiked wheels attached to the back of cowboy boots. Cowboys used the spurs to nudge their horse along.

Hands on the Trail

The rancher hired several men to round up cattle and drive them to the cattle town. Some cowboys worked on the ranch all year long, whereas others only worked on the trail drives. It took about seven to ten cowboys to watch over 1,000 head of cattle on the trail. With so many cattle to look after, every cowboy had an important role. Cowboys needed to locate themselves around the herd to keep the cattle moving together in the right direction and at the right speed.

wrangler with remuda

flank rider

drag riders

Drag riders rode behind the herd to keep the cattle moving.

Flank riders kept the herd from spreading out.

Wranglers were in charge of the **remuda**, or group of extra horses, taken on the trail drive. Wranglers made sure the horses in the remuda were rested, fed, and ready to take over for any tired horses.

The cook drove the chuck wagon.

swing rider

point rider

The trail boss was in charge of all the cowboys and cattle on the trail drive. He rode ahead of the herd to look for the next camp. He also kept track of lost animals.

Swing riders rode alongside the cattle to turn them in the right direction.

Point riders led the herd.

Just before four o'clock in the morning, Tom heard the cook's wake-up call. It was still dark outside, and Tom could barely move from his bed. Only two hours ago he was on the night watch, keeping an eye on the cattle and horses as they slept. The fifteen-hour workdays were starting to tire Tom.

While Tom and the other cowboys pulled on their pants and boots, the trail boss used a stick to draw a map on the ground of the fifteen-mile journey for the day. He marked the halfway point where they would meet the chuck wagon for lunch. Meanwhile, Tom and the others washed their face with water from the barrel by the chuck wagon. Tom hoped that the cold water would wake him up! After Tom packed his bedroll and placed it in the back of the chuck wagon, he started eating his breakfast. Mmmm...the coffee smelled good! The cattle were hungry, too. They grazed before they began their journey for the day.

At the first sight of daylight, the cowboys and cattle left camp. Tom liked traveling in the morning because it was still cool. He wondered if the cattle also preferred the morning because the dew was cool on their hooves. The herd would travel several hours before it would meet the wagon for lunch. The chuck wagon had already left earlier that morning.

Today, Tom was riding at the right side of the herd in the flank position. His job was to look for strays and keep the cattle moving at a slow pace. If the herd moved too quickly, the cattle would lose weight and not sell for a good price. Tom was glad he was not riding in the drag position because the cattle kicked up clouds of dust.

At bedtime, the cowboys rode in a circle around the herd to make the cattle lie down close to one another. Tom helped the wrangler **hobble** the horses by tying their front legs together so they could not wander away.

At nine o'clock, Tom finished his dinner. The trail boss had chosen several cowboys to work the night-watch shifts. Everyone set bedrolls around the fire by the chuck wagon. Tom watched the cook turn the front of the chuck wagon toward the North Star to help the trail boss know in which direction to travel in the morning. Meanwhile, Jake played his guitar and sang **cow lullabies** to lull the cattle to sleep and keep them calm. "O rest now, dogies, and breathe real slow. Tomorrow comes soon, and you'll be on the go."

THE CHUCK WAGON

The chuck wagon carried all the **chuck**, or food, for the trail drive. It also carried the supplies the cowboys needed. Four horses pulled the wagon, which was driven by the cook. The chuck wagon traveled ahead of the herd so the cook would have time to prepare food for the hungry cowboys.

Home away from home

The chuck wagon not only carried the supplies for the trip, it also made the cowboys feel at home. It was surrounded by delicious smells, held basic comforts like blankets and bandages, and was always waiting for them at the next stop. The cowboys gathered around the chuck wagon to eat and share songs and stories. When they ate together, they felt like a family.

A blanket or canvas could be stretched over the hoops.

The cook drove the wagon from a bench built near the front.

*A sling made of cowhide hung underneath the wagon. It held **cow chips** and wood for building fires. Cow chips are pieces of dried cow dung.*

A barrel of fresh water was attached to the side of the wagon. The cook refilled the barrel at a river or stream.

A coffee grinder, tin cups, pots, and pans hung on nails or hooks on the outside of the chuck box.

The back of the chuck box dropped down to become a table. The cook used this flat surface to do all of his food preparation such as rolling dough for pies.

The chuck box stored food and spices. Some drawers were filled with flour, sugar, dried fruit, beans, coffee, and tobacco. Other drawers held iron forks, spoons, knives, plates, and cups. A drawer called the **possible drawer** held castor oil, razors, and a sewing kit.

Large pots such as the **dutch oven** sometimes hung from a hook beneath the wagon.

A box called the **boot** held the pots and skillets.

FUEL FOR THE COWBOYS

Food for the trail drive had to last without spoiling during long, hot days. There was no refrigeration to keep it fresh. There were only a few foods that would not spoil, so cowboys ate the same kinds of meals over and over again. Meals were cooked over a campfire in a pot that hung from a pothook above the fire.

The wrangler helped the cook find and chop wood for the fire. When there was a shortage of wood, the wrangler collected dried cow dung for burning.

The cowboy's diet

Beans, bread and beef made up most of a cowboy's diet. Injured, sick, or dangerous cattle could not be sold at market so they were killed and eaten. Beef could not be kept for long before it spoiled. A dead cow was usually left to cool overnight and was cooked the next day. If an armadillo or a rattlesnake crossed the cook's path, it often ended up in a stew or chili. The cook always used a lot of spices to make the meals taste good.

Getting groceries

Before the trail drive, the cook had to stock the wagon with enough food to last one or two months. He could not go shopping during the drive because towns with stores were often too far away from the trails. On later trail drives, salesmen went out on the trail to sell the cook fresh provisions.

Preparing ahead

The cook had to be organized to feed all the hard-working cowboys. He left bread dough to rise for hours before he could bake it. He soaked dried beans in water overnight so he could boil them in the morning. The cook had to be sure that he was ready for each meal. He worked hard to keep the cowboys happy!

Making bread

The cook always had sourdough **starter** ready for making bread. Starter was a yeast,

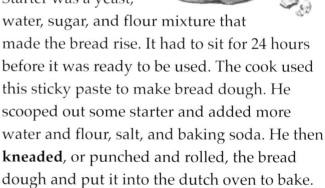

water, sugar, and flour mixture that made the bread rise. It had to sit for 24 hours before it was ready to be used. The cook used this sticky paste to make bread dough. He scooped out some starter and added more water and flour, salt, and baking soda. He then **kneaded**, or punched and rolled, the bread dough and put it into the dutch oven to bake.

Iron bars were laid across a fire pit, making a grate on which large pots sat. One end of the pit sloped up so burning embers could be shoveled out and used for the dutch oven.

Grocery list
* ★ garlic cloves ★ chili powder
* ★ yeast ★ dried fruit ★ sugar
* ★ beans ★ onions ★ flour
* ★ lard ★ potatoes

Mealtime

Cowboys ate in groups. Each group took a turn sitting around the chuck wagon while another group looked after the horses and cattle. The men ate quickly, knowing the next group was hungry, too. When they ate all they could, they scraped the leftovers into the fire and put their dirty dishes into a metal bucket for the cook to wash.

Sample trail menu
BREAKFAST: bread or biscuits, coffee
LUNCH: chili or stew, bread, water
SUPPER: steak and beans, potatoes
with gravy, biscuits,
water or coffee

pothook

Cooks baked pies, biscuits, breads, and cooked steaks in the dutch oven. The dutch oven was a large, heavy pot. Burning coals from the fire pit were placed under the dutch oven and on top of its lid. Heat from the top and bottom helped cook or bake the food evenly.

DANGERS ON THE TRAIL

Cowboys faced many dangers on the trail. The fear of wolves, bears, scorpions, and rattlesnakes kept them alert. Blizzards and lack of water also made life hard for the cowboys. The biggest danger they faced on the trail, however, was a **stampede**. During a stampede, frightened cattle ran off in all directions. Stampedes often occurred at night, when the cattle could not see what was around them. The first sign of a stampede was the loud, rumbling sound of hooves pounding against the ground.

Dangers of a stampede

When cattle stampeded, they ran close together, causing some cattle and horses to stumble and fall. Sometimes cowboys were knocked off their horses. Cowboys, horses, and cattle were often trampled under the feet of stampeding cattle. Many were hurt and even killed. At other times, stampeding cattle ran off cliffs or into rushing rivers. In one stampede, cattle ran into a gully and over 2,000 steers died or were lost!

A loss of money

Cattle ranchers lost money from accidents caused by stampedes. When cattle were lost or killed, there were fewer cattle to sell. Cattle that were bruised or had broken bones or horns were worth less money. Some cattle lost weight or looked frightened when they stampeded. If cattle came to a cattle town looking scared or skinny, people did not want to buy them.

Try your hand as a cowboy on the trail! The game on these two pages requires two or three players, a die, and a lot of courage! Roll the die and move a coin or other marker along the trail. Will you be the first to get your cattle to the cattle town?

Start the trail here.

Coyotes attack a cow. Lose 1 turn.

There was a snake in your boot, but you found it. Go ahead 1 space.

Cook helps you recover from an injury. Rest up for next turn.

Successful river crossing

Chuck wagon stuck in mud. Lose 1 turn.

Lullaby calmed cattle. No stampede. Move ahead 1 space.

Rustlers steal 100 head of cattle. Go back 3 spaces.

Bad Water

Some cowboys tried to pick up a coin from the ground while racing on a horse at top speed.

Cowboys worked hard, but they liked to have fun, too. They played games such as dominoes or cards. A game called "mumble-the-peg" was especially popular. Players flipped sharp wooden pegs into the ground and tried to get them to stand up straight. The loser had to pull his pegs out of the ground with his teeth!

Riding contests

To break up the routine of the trail drive cowboys competed in riding contests. These contests helped them practice handling horses and roping cattle. Contests also provided an opportunity to have some fun. Competition to see who was the best horseman was fierce!

Love songs and lullabies

Singing, humming, and whistling were part of the everyday life of cowboys. They used music to avoid boredom on the long trail drive. Some songs were sad, and some were cheerful. Cowboys also sang love songs. Some cowboys played instruments such as the harmonica, fiddle, or guitar. The cattle liked hearing songs, too. During the day, the cowboys sang to help move along the cattle that lagged behind.

Telling tall tales

After the sun went down and the supper dishes were cleared away, the cowboys gathered around the campfire to relax. They took turns telling **tall tales**. Tall tales are stories that are somewhat exaggerated. Have you ever told a tall tale? Tell one to your friends using as many details as you can so that your friends can visualize your story as you tell it.

> ♫ **A cowboy song** ♫
> All day on the prairie in a saddle I ride
> Not even a dog, boys, to trot by my side.
> My fire I kindle with chips gathered round
> And boil my own coffee without being ground.
> I wash in a puddle and wipe on a sack,
> I carry my wardrobe right here on my back.

ARRIVING AT THE CATTLE TOWN

The cattle trails ended at cattle towns such as Abilene and Dodge City, which were located at railheads. Cattle towns were also known as boomtowns because they boomed, or grew quickly in size and population. Many people in the boomtowns made money from the cattle business. Hotels, banks, offices, shops, and saloons opened to offer services to the people who visited and lived there. Cattle towns were busy when the cowboys arrived. The cowboys were paid $100 at the end of the trail drive and were ready to spend their money!

Selling the cattle

When they arrived in town, the cattle were kept in pens. Some were sold to people in town, and others were bought by **wholesalers**. Wholesalers are people who buy something at one price and sell it at a higher price. Cattle wholesalers made money by selling cattle in the big cities of the northeast. The cattle that were going to the cities were put into railroad cars. When they arrived, they were taken to **slaughterhouses** to be butchered. The beef was bought by shopkeepers, who then sold it to their customers.

Business in cattle towns

Everything a weary cowboy needed could be found in the cattle town. After months of sitting in the saddle and sleeping on the ground, cowboys were eager for a warm bed, a hot bath, and a good meal! They slept at a hotel and had a haircut and shave at the barbershop.

When cowboys came off the trail, their clothing was ragged and dirty. They needed new clothes. Shopkeepers stocked their shelves with shirts, pants, chaps, bandannas, leather boots, and cowboy hats of every shape and size—all the important items that a cowboy needed for his next trail drive.

Back to work

Some cowboys found work and stayed in the cattle towns. They loaded cattle into railway cars or helped look after the cattle that were not shipped to the slaughterhouses. Sometimes a cowboy learned a new job such as carpentry or bartending. Other cowboys traveled back to the ranches in the west to drive another herd along the trail.

Dressed in clean, new clothes, these cowboys were ready to have some fun! Every cattle town had a saloon where cowboys could gamble, listen to music, dance, and drink whiskey. Before going out, however, these cowboys dressed up in their new clothes and posed for a picture taken by a professional photographer.

OLD WEST PHOTO ALBUM

Photographers often made trips to the open range to take pictures of cowboys on the trail. The cowboys bought the pictures to keep or to send to friends and family in the east. The photographs on these pages were taken in the 1800s and early 1900s. The people in the photographs are actual cowboys who worked on the trail.

(above) At this roundup camp, the cook is making bread under a tent behind his chuck wagon.

(left) Cowboys took turns having supper so that some could eat while others watched over the herd of cattle.

(right) These cowboys took time out of their busy day on the trail to line up for a photograph.

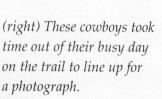

(above) The cook often took time out to give the cowboys a haircut and shave. Sometimes he had helpers.

(left) When a cowboy reached a cattle town, he bought new clothes and had his portrait taken. Cowboys liked to show off their equipment, such as their guns and lariats.

(below) The cattle town had large pens into which the cattle were driven. From here they were loaded into the railway cars along runways and ramps.

END OF THE TRAIL DRIVES

The open range allowed cattle to graze freely. By the late 1800s, however, people began to settle the land. Railways helped many areas grow quickly. Unsettled territories grew into towns and cities almost overnight.

Don't fence me out!

Cattle drives were unpopular with the settlers. They did not like cattle grazing on their pastures or bringing diseases to their livestock. They were fearful of stampedes that could destroy their farms and animals. To keep their farms safe, ranchers started putting up barbed-wire fences. Fencing made it difficult for cowboys to bring herds of cattle across the west. Many cattle trails were blocked by fences.

longhorn

Hereford

A different kind of cattle

Cattle ranchers began to raise Hereford cattle. Herefords had more beef and were ready to take to market sooner than longhorns. They had shorter legs and could not walk the long distance of the trail drives.

The end of an era

When the railways branched out across the west, ranchers no longer had to drive their cattle hundreds of miles to cattle towns. Trains made cattle drives unnecessary. By the end of the century, cattle drives were a thing of the past.

Wooden fences were expensive because wood was difficult to find on the plains. Wire fences were not expensive, but stampeding cattle easily broke through them. A barbed wire fence was more effective because it had sharp picks that hurt cattle when they tried to trample it.

GLOSSARY

barbed wire Fence wire that has sharp points

boomtown A town that grew quickly in population

branding The act of marking an animal's hide

bronco buster A cowboy who captures and tames wild horses

chuck wagon A wagon that carried food, supplies, and cooking equipment on trail drives

cow pony A horse that has been tamed

drag rider A cowboy who rides at the rear of a herd to keep it moving

dutch oven A large, covered pot that was heated from the bottom and the top

flank rider A cowboy who rides at the side of the herd to keep it from spreading out

mumble-the-peg A game played by tossing sharp, wooden pegs into the ground

open range A large area of open grazing land

point rider A cowboy who rides at the front of the herd on the trail drive

railhead The end of a railway line

remuda The extra horses taken on the trail drive

roundup The act of collecting and sorting cattle for a trail drive

stampede (n) An event in which startled cattle suddenly run in all directions

swing rider A cowboy who rides alongside a herd to turn it in the right direction

Texas fever A disease carried by ticks that infected and killed cattle

trail boss The cowboy in charge of all other cowboys and cattle on the trail drive

vaquero A Spanish or Mexican cowboy

wrangler The cowboy in charge of the remuda on the trail

INDEX

1 2 3 4 5 6 7 8 9 0   Printed in the U.S.A.   7 6 5 4 3 2 1 0 9 8